# DROPLETS IN AN EMPTY REED

## COLLECTION OF MUSES

AF536151

SUBASHREE VIJAYADEV

Copyright © Subashree Vijayadev
All Rights Reserved.

This book has been self-published with all reasonable efforts taken to make the material error-free by the author. No part of this book shall be used, reproduced in any manner whatsoever without written permission from the author, except in the case of brief quotations embodied in critical articles and reviews.

The Author of this book is solely responsible and liable for its content including but not limited to the views, representations, descriptions, statements, information, opinions and references ["Content"]. The Content of this book shall not constitute or be construed or deemed to reflect the opinion or expression of the Publisher or Editor. Neither the Publisher nor Editor endorse or approve the Content of this book or guarantee the reliability, accuracy or completeness of the Content published herein and do not make any representations or warranties of any kind, express or implied, including but not limited to the implied warranties of merchantability, fitness for a particular purpose. The Publisher and Editor shall not be liable whatsoever for any errors, omissions, whether such errors or omissions result from negligence, accident, or any other cause or claims for loss or damages of any kind, including without limitation, indirect or consequential loss or damage arising out of use, inability to use, or about the reliability, accuracy or sufficiency of the information contained in this book.

Made with ♥ on the Notion Press Platform
www.notionpress.com

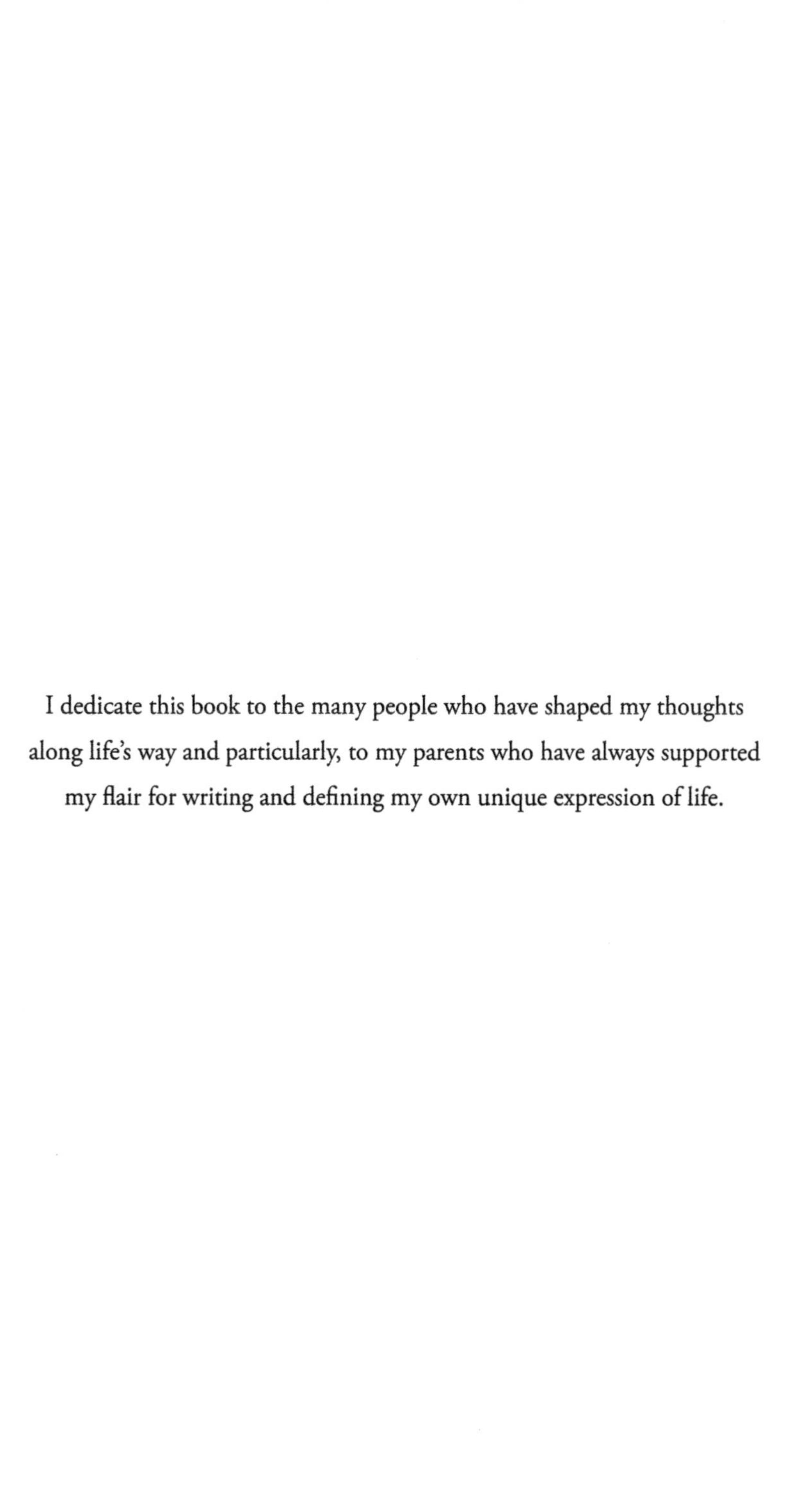

I dedicate this book to the many people who have shaped my thoughts along life's way and particularly, to my parents who have always supported my flair for writing and defining my own unique expression of life.

# Contents

# Preface

Each phase of life brings with it realizations that are relevant to our sense of self at that phase. They are strung together as a chain of realizations that shape ones newly emerging self. These realizations shape our identity and thus, our destinies.

The emphasis of this collection of muses is therefore upon the changing self, that with every new undertanding morphs into a new personality that views the world with a different perspective.

I hope these reflections of life will help clarify your understanding of apparently trivial things that have a big impact on our minds.

# 1. For What Purpose

Life is a changing canvas-
The strokes once bold
Now, blurred;
The dashes dainty-
Now, outstood.
The picture painted before
Was of a demure lass
That feared many a storm
And fancied many a charm.
Now, dignity deigned
To laugh at cares
And in occasional respite, laze.

With the picture altered
What remains is merely its semblance in shade.
Then for what purpose were we made
If we are thus altered?
Gently as the running brook that shapes the roughened rock,
Life makes the frivolous painting
A fervent masterpiece.

# 2. Recalling

I had forgotten the divine music
That once ran through me
And pulsated in ecstatic strains
In every one of my veins.
I had forgotten the joy that once
Surged through my heart
And urged me forward.
But how marvellously you roused me from my stupor
By gently tapping me till I wakened
And remembered
The glory of the light I am still;
The music that my spirit spells;
The joy that in my heart swells;
The shrine that my being dwells in.

# 3. A Hindu Marriage

Two hearts unite
In heavenly grace
And circle the
Sacred fire.
Seven steps of truth
And solemn rites
Bind the groom and bride.
A life of trust and truth,
Love and light,
Bowing to divine will;
They vow to walk
Their life anew
With patience and foresight.

# 4. Searching God

Oh idols, carved in human taste
In them do you reside?
Or in the streams that skip in haste
Beneath their ripples do you hide?
When the darkness dies at dawn
And the birds begin their song,
On the risen sun of morn,
Do you ride along?
When human hearts are held by love
And holy feelings felt,
Do you then descend from above?
And warm our hearts to melt?

# 5. Life, A Race!

Life, a marathon,
Runners racing shoulder to shoulder-
As I run, others race along with me.
Race, race towards our destinies…

One beside me stumbles- I slacken pace,
Reach out to pull him up,
But, I cannot tarry longer,
For I must race, race towards my destiny!
One another drops dead, I dart towards him
And stop in my tracks;
But I must lift myself yet again,
And join the rest;
For I must race, race towards my destiny!

As we race, the path is sometimes over spread with flowers;
Sometimes, coloured beams of light
Encircle our heads and feet;
Sometimes, falls of sparkling water
Dance before our eyes;
As we race, race towards our destinies…

But sometimes, the ground caves in,
And people fall by dozen into an abyss,
Yet the ones that jump the gorge

Must race, race towards their destinies…

Sometimes, darkness is all that one sees;
Sometimes, all eyes are dazed
Yet they must race, race towards their destinies…

A fellow racer who stumbled a while ago
Can barely stand now,
And lies flat on his back;
How long can I stand stricken,
Looking at his lifeless form?
I must race, race towards my destiny…

Many are the wondrous spectacles
Along the course;
Replete with laughter and sobs a many
Yet, forced to falter every step along the way;
All that matters is to race, race towards our destinies…

# 6. River of Change

Like the flowing river, we move on and on,
Changing paths and meandering our way
Through calm and storm;
Like the flowing waters, we change in colour and form.
What seemed good, is useless now,
What angered you once, now a mellow thought;
Years of resentment, disperse as mist,
What was once despised is now sought,
What was, is now lost.
We are but rivers of restless thought
That change in desire and state;
But also passive water and watchers
Of fate.

# 7. Sea Shore

I sit upon the sandy shores
And feel the evening air.
The waves rush forward in merry glee
And the sun has softened her glare.
My heart soars with the waves that rise
And revels in their golden gleam
For the waves remind me of hope
That hops in every daring dream.
But I seek not the waves that rise
For they are but bound earthward,
But the aspiring skies
They joyously leap toward.

# 8. Change

The vagaries of life unfold before your eyes-
Nothing is constant-
Except watching of them.
Stone hard confidence
Must soften in submission
There can be no solid stance,
For life is an uncertain dance.

# 9. Constancy

Where is constancy? Can it in human hearts be,
That pine in emotion
pressed by partial understanding-
Or whine in distress
dressed by delusion.
Back and forth
the heart oscillates, mind opines.
The thoughts born of such flickering
Can be no respite for suffering.
Constancy then can never be sought
In human ties
that sleep on tides that rise and fall.
Constancy is in the sun
whose glory gives the moon her beams
that in turn upturn the mighty seas.

# 10. Rain

The heavens resound with laughter-
Mirthful tears roll down.
Vain man's petty follies,
The Gods above look on.

# 11. Of Great and Small

The bud that opens into flower
Amazes me not,
But the bouquet in glitter paper
I happily sought.
But pray tell me, when the small
Fails to surprise,
Can the great, entice?
If the great can indeed lure me,
Can it greater than small, suffice?

# 12. Earthquake

Oh earth, your heart has broken
That you must see it fit
To vent your spleen upon poor folk.
Rumbles of anguish
That you could hide no more,
Has burst forth
To vanquish
Human hope-
As human lives upon you rest.

# 13. Meekness

Often that which lowers in humility
is unnoticed
But heightened in worth.
Fail not to marvel at the soil at your feet-
It is worthier than the flowers in the hair.

# 14. Beauty

Beauty is unmasked ugliness-
It flits on a smiling lip
And sleeps on a frown genuine.
But where the thoughts attempt to hide,
Beauty shall not reside.

# 15. Wisdom

Knowledge can be stale,
But wisdom never is.
Knowledge is the stagnant pool
Of placid water's bliss.
Borrowed drops may fetch you pride
Though it bears the names of all.
But surging from your emptiness
Is a wordless waterfall.

9 798889 757122

Printed by Libri Plureos GmbH in Hamburg, Germany